STEAMBOATS

Sara Wright

SHIRE PUBLICATIONS

Published in Great Britain in 2013 by Shire Publications Ltd,
Midland House, West Way, Botley, Oxford OX2 0PH, UK.

43-01 21st Street, Suite 220B, Long Island City, NY
11101, USA.

E-mail: shire@shirebooks.co.uk   www.shirebooks.co.uk

A CIP catalogue record for this book is available from the
British Library.

Shire Library no. 681.   ISBN-13: 978 0 74781 141 1

Sara Wright has asserted her right under the Copyright,
Designs and Patents Act, 1988, to be identified as the
author of this book.

Designed by Tony Truscott Designs, Sussex, UK
and typeset in Perpetua and Gill Sans.

Printed in China through Worldprint Ltd.

13 14 15 16 17   10 9 8 7 6 5 4 3 2 1

COVER IMAGE
The *Belle of Calhoun*, built at St. Louis in 1895. The boat
was sunk, raised, and repaired three times over her life,
until being burned during the winter of 1930–31.

TITLE PAGE IMAGE
View from the bluffs above the Ohio River, near Cincinnati
in 1913.

CONTENTS PAGE IMAGE
Postcard image from about 1919, showing the sidewheel
excursion steamboat *J.S.* at a landing on the Mississippi
River. The boat was owned by the Streckfus Steamboat
Company of St. Louis.

ACKNOWLEDGEMENTS
For the patience of my friends and family; for Gay Wands
who made this opportunity known to me; for Wayne and
Jean who told me the truth; for the kind assistance of the
late Henry R. Burke of Marietta, Ohio; for Dave whose
kind consideration and encouragement was, and remains,
invaluable; to my editor, Kelli Christiansen, who patiently
guided me along the path to bring this little project to life;
and to the Dresden Belle, a ten-year love that gave birth
to a life-long interest ... and this little book.

PHOTOGRAPH ACKNOWLEDGEMENTS
Cover art, The Betsy Ann by Dean Cornwell, c. 1930.
Permission for use of this image kindly given by Jeff Spear
and the Sons & Daughters of Pioneer Rivermen, Marietta,
Ohio. Images on pages 43, 51, and 52 (top) courtesy of
The S&D Reflector and the collection of Captain "Doc"
Hawley. Images on pages 5, 27, 28 (both), 34 (top),
37 (top), 38, and 52 from the personal collection of
G. David Thomson. Image on page 8 courtesy of the
Indianapolis Museum of Art, gift of Jerry M. Wright.
Image on page 20 courtesy of the University of Chicago
Library, Special Collections Research Center. Images
on page 29 courtesy of the Postal Museum,
Smithsonian Institution. Images on pages 24 and 30
courtesy of the Smithsonian American Art Museum, Gifts of
Mrs. Joseph Harrison, Jr. Image on page 45 courtesy of the
Louisiana State University Museum of Art. Images on pages
22 and 23 courtesy of the National Information Service for
Earthquake Engineering, EERC, University of California,
Berkeley. Images Courtesy of the Library of Congress: page
5, LC-D4-33072; page 6 (top) LC-USZ62-46966, (bottom)
LC-DIG-ppmsca-05403; page 12 LC-USZ62-102509; page
15, LC-USZC4-5945; pages 16-17, LC-D4-22603; page 17,
LC-USZ62-110384; page 24, LC USZ62-102509; page 31,
LC-USZC4-3168; pages 32-33, LC-D418-8120; page 40
(lower left) LC-DIG-cai2a15427; page 43 (top)
LC-DIG-cwpbh-03683; pages 46-47, LC-D4-34341;
pages 60-61, LC-D4-73472. Images on pages 26 (bottom),
29, 34 (bottom), 44, 50, and 59 (top) from the Inland Rivers
Collection of The Public Library of Cincinnati and Hamilton
County. Image on page 36 courtesy of the Rubenstein
Library, Broadside Collection, Duke University. Images
on pages 7 and 11 courtesy Alamy, Ltd. Photographs on
pages 57 and 58 by the author. All other images from the
personal collection of the author.

Shire Publications is supporting the Woodland Trust, the UK's leading woodland conservation charity, by funding the dedication of trees.

CONTENTS

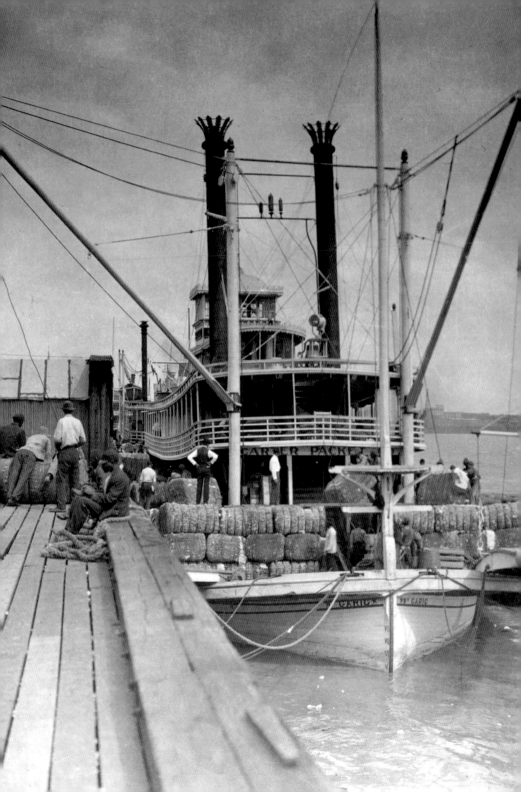

CONFLUENCE

THE IMAGE of the American steamboat cruising the rivers is one that excites the imagination. With a white superstructure gleaming in the sun, woodwork like lace trim on a summer gown, and smoke curling from the stacks like tangled black hair, the sound of her steam whistles could be heard from as far as 5 miles away. Each of those whistles had its own voice, the timbre and tone of which made their calls identifiable, a siren song, luring many with the promise of adventure and a better life.

Enthralled by such a romantic image, it would be easy to forget the role played by the steamboats and their hard-working crews to open the way for settlers of the American West. While the temptation to rely on the image is great, the reality was far richer and infinitely more rewarding.

No sooner had the ink dried on the Peace of Paris in 1783, officially ending the American Revolution, than the new country found itself embroiled in a second revolt, which was to determine how the states were to be organized and governed as a nation. With the treaty, England ceded additional territory to the new nation, virtually doubling its size. As the states juggled and negotiated among themselves to maintain their autonomy, they also sought to claim a share of those territories. However, the nation's leaders, among them Thomas Jefferson, Alexander Hamilton, and James Monroe, wanted control of the land because it was seen as a source of revenue, both to finance the government and to pay the debts incurred fighting the Revolution.

The Philadelphia Convention was assembled in 1787 to address the weaknesses in the Articles of Confederation, but it rapidly turned into an event that changed the course of the nation. After a great deal of difficult negotiations, agreement was eventually reached, resulting in the U.S. Constitution. The Constitution did not immediately bring peace to the land, however, as representatives of the various states, factions, and groups, reasonable men as well as villains, sought to stretch the intent of the document to suit their own ends. Although difficult, tumultuous years followed, it was an era vibrant with opportunity, attracting people of intellect, enthusiasm, and conviction. All of them sought to make their

Opposite:
A Mississippi River packet, tied at a New Orleans wharf, about 1910. Note the guards, which extend well beyond the width of the hull (beam), increasing storage space for cargo.

5

Mandan Bullboat, photograph by Edward S. Curtis. Native Americans as well as settlers used these boats, made from buffalo skins stretched over willow frames. The hair on the hides kept the boats from spinning in the water.

fortunes; all of them helped to open the way west.

People had begun moving inland in the mid-1750s, into the Kentucky territory through the Cumberland Gap and from New England into Pennsylvania and the Ohio territory. By 1780, the population of the Kentucky area was 500,000 people, while that of Pennsylvania was approximately 300,000. However, that was a mere trickle compared to the unstoppable stream of people who began migrating over the Allegheny and Appalachian mountains after the Treaty of Paris was signed.

The rivers were the country's first highways into the interior. Whether to move to a new settlement or to take the harvest to market, going by water was easier, took less time, and was less hazardous than going overland. Of course, Native Americans had for centuries routinely used these streams to travel the waterways via bullboats and canoes. Since 1698, the French had traveled the Missouri and Mississippi rivers hunting for furs, which they took down to the port at New Orleans, and then sold back to Europe.

George Napper's keelboat and crew at dinner at Givens Landing, West Virginia, circa 1872.

George Nappers Boat & Crew at dinner at Givens Landing

Colonists used everything from dugout canoes to rafts, flatboats, keelboats, and barges to move themselves across the country. Gradually they worked their way downstream, settling wherever the resources would be sufficient to their needs. People who settled further inland generally farmed only enough to support their families, while those closer to the rivers quickly began to seek outside markets; as soon as the farmers and tradesmen in the area had any surplus crops and merchandise, they returned to the river, offering their produce to settlements downstream, inevitably arriving at Natchez, Mississippi, then New Orleans.

The settlers constructed what was, in effect, a large, rectangular, floating box generally about 60 to 75 feet long by 15 to 20 feet wide, with freeboard (sides) 6 feet deep, which would then leave 3 feet above the waterline when laden. When the hull was completed and its seams caulked with oakum, the builders would turn the hull into the water right side up, at which point wide planks were laid side by side to create a deck. On the first boats, only a rude shelter was constructed to protect the crew from the elements; a sand pit was built to provide warmth and to cook food. An entryway into the hull was accessed by a ladder, where cargo was carefully placed to evenly distribute its weight. A long spar with a paddle on the end was installed at the rear of the boat to be used as a rudder, with other spars at each side, and perhaps a smaller one at the front. The crews generally consisted of about five men, most frequently the boat's owner, a pilot who knew the river, and three men to work the oars, who usually were family members, neighbors, or friends of the owner.

The flatboats sent by the settlers carried just about everything: flour, whiskey, rope, corn, apples, potatoes, dried peaches, salt-cured pork, livestock, glass, pottery, furniture—whatever was manufactured or grown that could be sent without rotting was packed for sale.

President Thomas Jefferson encouraged this westward migration. He was a man of expansive vision who also acted to bring that vision to stunning reality. He wanted to establish United States's control over the Northwest and Louisiana territories to avoid those areas being reclaimed by Spanish, French, and English interests, which were a constant threat to the new country's stability and progress. The French had laid claim to the Missouri River area north of St. Louis since about 1686, while the Spanish held the areas of Texas, Arkansas, and Florida. Both countries alternated their hold on the Louisiana area over the years, transferring their authority back and forth as neither country was able to make the settlement pay financially. The penultimate transfer took place in 1762, when the French gave the New Orleans port area back to Spain.

As long as the Spanish held control of New Orleans and the Louisiana territory, American boatmen were able to do business at the port, selling their wares and produce. Although wary of the each other's motives, the Spanish and the Americans had developed a symbiotic relationship that served their mutual needs: During the Revolution, the Spanish had traded with the Americans, selling gunpowder and other supplies for their fight against the English, a mutual enemy, while the flatboats brought the flour and wheat the Spanish needed. After the war, dissention arose because the Americans assumed they had free access to the Natchez and

As President Thomas Jefferson's expansionist vision resulted in the Louisiana Purchase of 1803. The development of the steamboat was a great influence in bringing immigrants into the territory and unifying its far-flung settlements.

The Jolly Flat Boat Men, hand-colored mezzotint by Thomas Doney, 1847, after George Caleb Bingham, 1845. Although initially a portrait painter, Bingham is perhaps best known for scenes showing settlers' life along the Mississippi and Missouri rivers.

New Orleans riverfronts, forgetting that the Spanish had not signed the Treaty of Paris. Eventually, another agreement was reached in 1793, the Treaty of San Lorenzo, which allowed American control of the Natchez district and use of the Port of New Orleans.

Spanish colonial governors, worried about American insurgence into the territory, attempted to control the settlement by requiring that American boatmen sign loyalty oaths indicating their intent to become Spanish subjects. In addition to making certain that the boatmen behaved well, the merchant boatmen told their crews to go along with the governors' requests, avoid any quarrels, and pay bribes as needed to ease their relations with the Spanish officials. In this way, trade flourished and everyone profited from the arrangement. By the time of the Louisiana Purchase, fully 15 percent of the nation's trade went through the New Orleans port.

Jefferson did not believe the nation's interests were threatened with Spanish control over the territory. But after Spain again returned it to France in 1802, he was afraid that U.S. access to the Gulf of Mexico and the oceans beyond would be cut off. When Jefferson learned that Napoleon was interested in selling the territory to pay for his military campaigns, he pounced. The American Minister to France, John Livingston, eventually purchased the entire Louisiana territory for $15 million, nearly doubling the size of the United States.

Previously, with the creation of the U.S. Customs Service in 1789, Congress had established official ports of entry to collect duties, which were used by the government to build its infrastructure. Trade had increased along the rivers to such an extent that the first official inland port of entry was established by Congress at Louisville in 1789, then with other towns over the years as trade in the areas increased. This increase spoke to the need for an improved method of transportation.

Boat builders in the Ohio Valley had initially constructed the schooners with which they were familiar. Meant for ocean travel, the ships frequently became stranded on sandbars and speared by the snags of trees. The Ohio River was essentially navigable only during the spring and fall by flatboats and keelboats, after rains upriver produced freshets that raised the water level. Something else was needed: a vessel suited to the varying depths of the streams and their winding routes through the American landscape.

Flatboatmen are shown in this undated photograph, pulling their vessel through river shallows.

INNOVATION

DURING THE COURSE of bringing the steamboat to reality, many men flirted with the idea with little success; others paid it earnest courtship only to have their efforts break apart and sink away beneath their feet.

In 1707, Denis Papin of Germany, who had earlier demonstrated the power of steam pressure to push the lid off a pot, created what we know as the pressure cooker, which led to the development of the steam-release valve, preventing explosions of Papin's cooker. The valve, in turn, led to the later development of the piston-driven steam engine.

While James Watt is generally considered as the inventor of the steam engine, that credit more correctly should be attributed to Thomas Newcomen, whose development of a piston-driven engine in 1712 was an improvement upon the invention of a pump by Thomas Savery. That pump, introduced in 1698, used steam to force ground water out of coal mines, allowing workers to dig deeper for coal. However, the volumes of water that needed to be moved could not be accommodated by Savery's pump. The amount of heat required to produce sufficient steam caused the device's soldered joints to melt. In order to produce enough steam, the engineer would circumvent the pressure release valve, causing the overheated vessel to explode due to the expansion of the vapor within.

The potential hazards, the costs for fuel, and the number of machines and workers required to keep the mines dry was so prohibitive that Savery's pump languished until Newcomen's introduction of a much safer version. Newcomen, one of Savery's employees, along with his neighbor, John Calley, developed a steam-driven piston for the pump.

Savery had dispensed with Papin's piston when he created his pump. Newcomen returned to it, adding the steam piston to increase the pump's strength. However, the danger of explosion affected their machine, too. When Newcomen and Calley increased the steam pressure, heat from the fire caused the lead solder to melt, allowed cold water to enter the cylinder, and spewed pressurized, scalding water. The two men realized that the force of steam pressure might be used to their advantage. In 1712, they adapted the pump to allow a stream of water to enter the cylinder once every cycle, just as it reached its full head of steam. The resulting pump was an outstanding success, its use spreading across Europe with demands for ever-increasing sizes of brass cylinders, making Newcomen a very successful man.

Newcomen pumps had been in production for more than twenty years when a model of the engine was brought to James Watt for repair. Employed at Glasgow University as an instrument maker, Watt saw that the constant heating and cooling of the piston cylinder wasted energy because it required the single cylinder be kept both hot and cold at the same time, a virtually impossible task. Watt created a separate condenser to inject cooler water into the cylinder, so that its heat could be maintained. The steam was then easily and efficiently cooled, allowing the piston to function smoothly.

For two years Watt experimented to produce an effective seal between the piston and cylinder, without success. While in London in 1769 to receive Patent No. 913 for his engine, Watt met with Matthew Boulton, a metals manufacturer. Together, the two men perfected the engine using the Wilkinson cylinders, beginning production in 1775. The Boulton & Watt engine rapidly became the standard of the time.

James Watt received a patent acknowledging his work developing an original idea thanks to the passage in England in 1624 of a law that granted inventors the right to protection of their original concepts and prototypes. Inventors in the United States did not enjoy such opportunities until 1790 when, after provisions for the initial patent act were established by the Constitution, the first Committee for the Encouragement of Useful Arts was assembled in Philadelphia. After his mission to Paris as Washington's first foreign secretary was completed, Thomas Jefferson's first assignment was as the new head of the committee to review inventors' requests for patents. Among the four applicants for the nation's first patents were James Rumsey and John Fitch, the American men most often credited with creating precursors to Robert Fulton's steamboat, *The North River* (i.e., *Clermont*). They had been competing many years for supremacy of their work, often accusing each other of plagiarism and deceit in excoriating printed statements. Their contentious situation was not helped by the fact that the first effort to issue patents was itself a work in progress, resulting in Jefferson ordering that all four applicants be awarded patents.

Thomas Newcomen (1664–1729) developed a steam engine in 1710 that was the first practical pump to remove ground water from coal mines. His adaptations of work by Thomas Savery and Denis Papin led to James Watt's development of a steam engine that could be used for applications other than collieries.

Robert Fulton (1765–1815), credited with developing the first commercially successful steamboat, also built the first practical submarine, the *Nautilus*, as well as early versions of naval torpedoes.

Before the Patent Acts were passed in 1793, inventors were required to submit proposals to their state legislatures to be awarded monopolies for their inventions, which would allow them exclusive rights for a specified number of years, during which no other competitors were allowed to use the invention. This meant that an inventor might claim the monopoly in one state while rights to a similar, competing invention could be claimed in another state by someone else. It is in this situation James Rumsey and John Fitch found themselves during the 1780s and 1790s.

Rumsey enjoyed financial and personal backing over the years. Early on, he built a boat with a wheel in the bow that worked poles to pull the boat upstream. With George Washington's recommendation, he was awarded a monopoly from the Virginia legislature for his boats. Discouraged with the first boat, Rumsey began work to develop a tubular boiler, using a theory credited earlier to Daniel Bernoulli. Rumsey wanted the boiler to produce enough steam to power a pump to propel water at high force from a pipe to drive the boat forward. After a lot of work to surmount problems with the intake on the pump, Rumsey's boat made a successful demonstration in late 1787, fully twenty years before Fulton launched *The North River*.

John Fitch had launched his steam-powered boat in August 1787, four months earlier than Rumsey. A silversmith and watchmaker by trade, Fitch had heard about Watt's engine, but as none was available in America, he and a friend, Henry Voight, worked to recreate one of their own. Their 45-foot boat was successful, its steam engine being used to power a series of connected, oar-like paddles that functioned much like men paddling a canoe. The following year, Fitch built a larger boat that he was able to run on the Delaware River between Philadelphia and Burlington, New Jersey, taking passengers and freight between the two towns. Unfortunately, Fitch was unable to sustain the route because of his poor business sense and was forced to abandon it.

It was at this time that Fitch and Rumsey began their pitched battle over exactly who had first invented the steamboat. When Jefferson ordered all four inventors be awarded patents, Fitch had a fit of pique and said he would go to England to patent Rumsey's steam boiler. Rumsey's backers sent him to England, where his engaging personality won him influential friends. Boulton and Watt were interested in using their engines to power a boat of Rumsey's design. However, Rumsey felt the contract was written entirely in favor of the two manufacturers, and he passed on the opportunity. In 1792, just before his newest boat, the *Columbia Maid*, was to be launched, Rumsey died, possibly from a cerebral aneurysm. He left behind drawings and plans, as well as several patents, for items that had to do with fluid power engineering, including a water turbine.

"Poor John Fitch," thoroughly disenchanted with the results of the first patent application process that had awarded patents to all four applicants, was unable to get additional backing. It was left to a charming, ambitious artist from Lancaster, Pennsylvania, named Robert Fulton, who had gone to England to study painting with Benjamin West, to bring the steamboat to fruition, combining the engine with a boat whose structure could support the functions of the engine.

John Fitch's steamboat was replicated, as shown in this July 1938 photograph, for the Marine Parade in Philadelphia Harbor.

Fulton arrived in London in 1790, full of confidence in his artistic skills. During the mid-eighteenth through early nineteenth centuries, England was undergoing what was described as "a frenzy of canal building." Fulton traveled all over the island to observe the canals, drawing inspiration for a system of "feeder" canals that would connect smaller towns with larger cities. He soon began proselytizing his system to anyone who would listen. No one stepped forward to finance the scheme, so Fulton moved on to other ideas.

On a trip to France in 1797, Fulton met with Napoleon Bonaparte with a proposal to build canals. When that effort collapsed, he met with government officials to seek funding to develop and build a "diving boat" intended for the defense of the French army from the British navy. That the idea was based on the *American Turtle*, a submarine concept originated and built in 1776 by David Bushnell, did not concern Fulton. He never claimed to have originated any of the devices he presented. A logical thinker, he examined the work of other people, freely adapting their ideas to his own, making practical changes as he saw fit. His work was exact; he built models to work out and test concepts, to be certain they performed as intended.

In 1802, Fulton was introduced to Robert Livingston. Like many wealthy men of his time, Livingston passed his time in the invention of items. Unfortunately, he was a man whose hand-eye coordination was limited to cutting the meat on his dinner plate; he had no talent for drawing and no training in the use of hand tools. He hired people to bring his ideas into existence, often changing his mind without any understanding of the difficulties he created for his workmen.

Livingston's foray into the development of his own steamboat concept in 1798 resulted in a craft so unwieldy and flimsy that the boat could neither support the weight nor survive the movement and vibration of the engine. The vessel literally broke away under the feet of Livingston and his engineer, Nicholas Roosevelt. Despite Livingston's constant changes and his niggardly attitude toward expenses required to build a more sturdy craft, he blamed Roosevelt for the boat's failure. However, before they could resolve their disagreements and undertake corrections, Jefferson sent Livingston to Paris and the project was abandoned.

After Fitch abandoned his steamboat project and left New York for Kentucky, Livingston sought the monopoly for himself. It was awarded to him in 1798, after Fitch's death, and would run for twenty years, provided he produce a boat before March 27, 1799, that could travel upstream on the Hudson River at the rate of 4 miles per hour. Livingston's first task upon his return to America was to see whether that monopoly had expired. It had, but his great wealth and political influence enabled him to have it extended.

Fulton built a model, for which Livingston suggested he use paddle wheels mounted vertically on the sides of the boat, a feature Roosevelt had

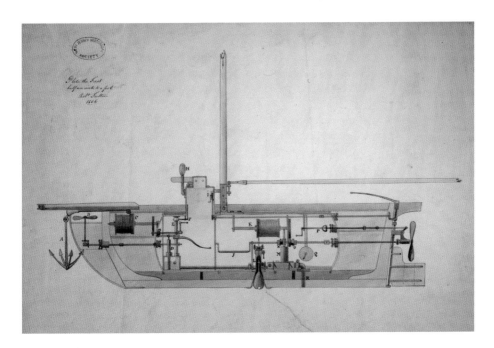

suggested for their earlier effort and which Livingston stubbornly rejected. Fulton blocked off a stream to test the model and, when its success was reported, Livingston authorized his purchase of a Boulton & Watt steam engine to be sent to America. Fulton returned to America in 1806, after a stop-off in England to order the engine.

Fulton was quite a different man than the one who left almost twenty years earlier. The years spent among the wealthy, educated, and influential men of the time paid unforeseen dividends. In Fulton's polished manner and confidence, people saw someone they felt would follow through with his intentions. While he indulged in self-aggrandizement and exaggerated the capacities of his inventions, he was also a man who observed, one who learned from his mistakes and those of others to achieve his own successes. Fulton had connected and corrected the theories of those who had gone before him, resulting in the steamboat *The North River*, often referred to as the *Clermont*.

Fulton's work paid off on a summer evening in 1807 when friends and supporters gathered on the bank of the Hudson River at New York City to board *The North River* steamboat. It had taken Fulton just six months to have the boat built according to his plans and with the Boulton & Watt engine. It was 150 feet long, with a beam of 13 feet. According to Fulton's notes, *The North River* made its way up the river to Livingston's estate, then

Fulton's drawings, such as this for the *Nautilus*, show his attention to detail in the development of his ideas, which included the construction of small models and prototypes to test his concepts.

went on to Albany, averaging 5 miles per hour, accomplishing in sixty hours a journey that would otherwise have taken a week on a wind-powered craft.

Fulton at first struggled to make the boat profitable. But once he began advertising its availability after the inaugural trip, people began to travel on his boat. At the end of the year, Fulton was able to report to Livingston that, after expenses, the boat had made a 5 percent profit. Over the winter, *The North River* was overhauled, resulting in a larger, more stable vessel. The additional investment paid off because the following year Fulton made enough money for himself and his partners to plan for additional boats, as well as for the boat that would open the western rivers, expanding the country's trade opportunities and providing a way for people to ride the river into the future.

A replica of Fulton's first successful steamboat, *The North River*, is shown at anchor during commemorative celebrations in 1909.

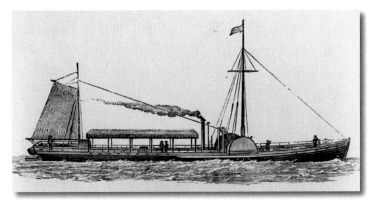

Detail from an advertisement of 1807, promoting transportation on *The North River*.

THE NEW ORLEANS

THE NEW ORLEANS began her life on the banks of the Monongahela River near Pittsburgh, Pennsylvania. Boat builders, migrating from New England into the Ohio River Valley in the 1750s, had quickly taken advantage of the vast old-growth forests lining the rivers, establishing boatyards amid the abundant stands of white oak, yellow pine, and black walnut trees. A number of yards built schooners for the sea trade, sending the boats to New Orleans and beyond to sail the world's oceans. The success of this enterprise was short-lived, however, due to political considerations and the variable depth of the Ohio River. The yards increasingly turned to building keelboats and flatboats with shallow hulls that were not as dependent on the spring and fall rains to maintain adequate depth for their passage. It was at one of these yards where the flatboat Nicholas Roosevelt used for his reconnaissance of the rivers was made, the same place he had *The New Orleans* built, the first steamboat to ply the Ohio and Mississippi rivers.

Before Chancellor Robert Livingston was sent to Paris by President Jefferson in 1799, he and Roosevelt were involved in a failed partnership to build a steamboat. Fulton and Livingston made Roosevelt a partner in the Mississippi Steamboat Navigation Company, in part because of this earlier legal obligation, assigning Roosevelt to make a survey of the Ohio and Mississippi rivers to check the feasibility of taking a boat to the City of New Orleans. He began this voyage in October 1810 with his young wife, Lydia Latrobe, the daughter of Benjamin Henry Latrobe, the country's first trained architect and civil engineer. Speed was not the object of the voyage; the currents, topography, and available resources on the rivers were all of concern. The six months Roosevelt spent on this survey resulted in a report that pleased his partners, with work beginning on the new boat not long after.

Although no definitive drawings of the boat survive, it is assumed *The New Orleans* was patterned after *The North River*, with some alterations made to accommodate the different conditions. She had a rounded hull 148 feet in length, with a 34.5-foot beam (width) and 12-foot draft (depth). Her engine

Opposite:
A replica of *The New Orleans* was built in 1911 for a commemorative voyage along the Ohio and Mississippi rivers, with celebrations held at riverfront towns to mark the 100th anniversary of the steamboat on western rivers.

Bond and pilot permit for the Falls-of-the-Ohio, issued to Davis Floyd, signed by William Henry Harrison, then governor of the Indiana territory. So many boats and lives had been lost on the rapids that only bonded pilots were permitted to guide the vessels over the falls.

and boilers were placed inside the hull, amidships, to power a pair of paddlewheels hung from each side. She had one stack, two masts, a bowsprit, and berths for 75 passengers. However, only Roosevelt, his pregnant wife, and their daughter Rosetta, as well as the boat's two pilots, crew, and maids were on board. When the boat departed from the Pittsburgh riverbank on October 11, 1811, plenty of people had shown up to wish them well, but most did not expect to see the boat again, believing it did not have enough power to make the return trip against the powerful currents of the river. While Nicholas and Lydia Roosevelt themselves had faith in their mission, as the boat disappeared downriver and the smoke from her stacks faded into the sky, they likely had very little notion of the adventure to come.

Rainfall in the region had been so sparse that there was not enough clearance for the boat to navigate the Falls-of-the-Ohio, a section of rapids more than 2 miles long that prevented all but the most skilled pilots from attempting to navigate its hazards. So many lives and cargos had been lost

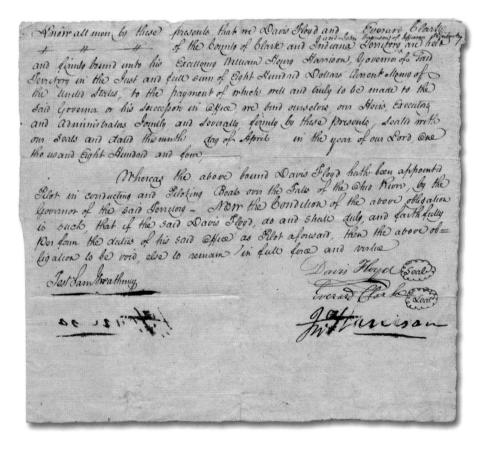

that the governing authorities required all boats to have a specially licensed pilot take them through the rapids. While Roosevelt and his crew awaited rainfall that would allow passage over the falls, Lydia gave birth to their second child, Henry Latrobe Roosevelt, on October 30, 1811. Nicholas passed the days giving rides for $1 to skeptics who did not believe the boat had the power to travel upstream, on one occasion taking the boat upriver to Cincinnati. Finally, in early December, enough rain had fallen to allow *The New Orleans* a 5-inch clearance for her hull against the bottom of the falls. Leaving the children with their nurse, the Roosevelts and their crew took the boat upstream to build speed before entering the thrashing waters. In a ride that must have felt like an eternity, *The New Orleans* made a successful run of the rapids, bobbing and settling in calmer waters about forty-five minutes later at the river landing of Shippingport. All aboard felt that the biggest obstacle had been passed, and they continued toward the settlement at Henderson, more than 200 miles downriver.

Each evening, the crew of *The New Orleans* tied the boat to trees or anchored close to the riverbank so they could go ashore to chop wood for fuel and to hunt for food. One night, everyone was awakened by what they thought was the boat being hit by a floating tree because it shuddered so badly. It was an earthquake, one of many they would experience over the coming weeks. Safer on the boat than on land, they proceeded to Henderson, where they found many chimneys had been knocked down by the quake.

The New Orleans was stocked with coal at Yellow Banks and went on its way. With nearly another 200 miles remaining before they entered the Mississippi River, and with virtually no settlements after New Madrid, they wanted to be sure of having enough fuel and food to last until they could stop safely to cut additional wood.

The beautiful primeval forest lining the river was falling away before their eyes, splintered trunks, massive root balls, and lurching limbs threatening the hull and paddles of the boat. *The New Orleans* was not the only vessel on the river; she shared the currents with flatboats, keelboats, barges, and other varied craft, often shouting

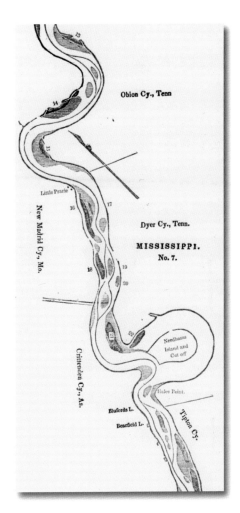

Chart by Samuel Cummings showing the New Madrid area of the Mississippi River. After leaving Henderson, New Madrid was the last settlement *The New Orleans* would see before reaching Natchez, more than 525 miles downriver.

The United States and surrounding countries are shown on this 1813 map. The central line shows the western edge of the Louisiana Purchase and boundaries of Spanish-held territories.

greetings back and forth as they met and passed each other on their way downstream. They shouted questions about their route; *The New Orleans*'s pilot, Andrew Jack, navigated according to landmarks learned over years of taking flatboats down the Mississippi. All of those were gone, as were many of their fellow travelers, shards of broken boats and barrels indicating the fates of so many other people who were caught in the sulphurous maelstrom.

It was decided to follow the main channel as much as possible, finally reaching the New Madrid settlement on December 19. The Roosevelts' first trip with the flatboat had taken six months and provided adventures of its own, but this one, while taking half as long to travel the 1,900 miles, must have seemed much longer.

One night the boat was tied at the down-stream end of Island No. 32 on the Mississippi River, safe from floating debris. During the night, those on board felt the boat shudder from what felt like trees hitting and rolling under *The New Orleans*'s hull. When they awoke the following morning, they thought the boat was adrift on the river but found, instead, that the island had disintegrated during the night, sinking away

Item from a local newspaper of the time reporting the arrival of *The New Orleans* on January 12, 1812.

The Louisiana Gazette
AND
DAILY ADVERTISER.

MONDAY MORNING, JANUARY 13.

We were late on Saturday politely favoured with Baltimore papers to the 14th ult, from which we make extracts.

The Steam Boat *New Orleans*, from Pittsburg, arrived here on Friday evening last. The captain reports that she has been *under way* not more than 259 hours from Pittsburg to this place, which gives about eight miles each hour.

The *New Orleans* steam Boat was built at Pittsburg by the Ohio Steam Boat company, under the patent granted to Messrs. Livingston and Fulton of New York. She is intended as a regular trader between this and Natchez, and will, it is generally believed, meet the most sanguine expectations of the company.

beneath them. The boat, still tied to the trees, was freed only when the hausers were cut with an axe. Nicholas Roosevelt made a note to tell river chronicler Zadoc Cramer that Island 32 "was no more."

They steamed on, finally arriving at Natchez on December 30, 1811, and continued to the City of New Orleans, where they were greeted with ceremony by city officials and townfolk on January 12, 1812. The Roosevelts left *The New Orleans* to begin packet service at the town for which she was named.

The New Orleans had been the first steamboat to navigate the Ohio and Mississippi rivers; she had been the first upon which a child had been born; she was the first to navigate the Falls-of-the-Ohio; and she had taken her passengers and crew safely through the Great Earthquake. Early in the morning of February 14, 1814, just over two years after she began her service, the packet *New Orleans* was leaving the riverbank at Baton Rouge when she was stabbed by a snag, becoming possibly the first steamboat to fall victim to the river, a "cause of death" that was to become ubiquitous in the coming years.

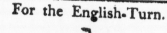

For the English-Turn.

THE STEAM-BOAT
New-Orleans

WILL run from this place to the English-Turn and back, on Friday next; to start precisely 10 A M — Tickets of admission may be procured at the two Coffee-Houses, at Three Dollars each The Boat it is expected, will return at 3 o'clock, P. M All Passengers, therefore, who may desire to dine before that hour, it is expected will carry with them their own provisions.
January 16

Above: Advertisement for *The New Orleans* listing her schedule and passage fares for trade between the City of New Orleans and Natchez, Mississippi.

Left: The Red River had a mass of driftwood so large it formed a floating island about 160 miles long. Using several snag boats he designed for the task, it took Shreve and his men five years to break up the "raft."

BUILDING A LEGACY

STEAMBOAT structure and mechanics evolved greatly during the first forty years of the boats' existence on the American waterways. The boats were adapted to meet the demands of the vast territory into which they traveled and the variety of the cargos they carried. As with *The New Orleans*, the first boats were constructed using techniques and practices that had proved successful in the deep waters of the world's oceans, meaning the boats were more likely to become stranded on river shoals and sandbars and more easily pierced by submerged hazards such as trees and boulders.

A former keelboat pilot, Henry Shreve is most often credited with creating the first flat-bottomed steamboat hulls. His many years of experience guiding keelboats through the hazardous twists and turns of the Mississippi River made him acutely aware of the shortcomings of the "fire canoes." He was captain of a steamboat built by Daniel French, the *Enterprise*, which in 1815 became the first steamboat to navigate upstream from New Orleans to Louisville. Shreve knew that the deeper-hulled boats, including the *Enterprise*, would never be successful on the western rivers.

The first boat Shreve built, the *Washington*, shared the more shallow lines of a keelboat, but did not vary substantially from the rounded hulls of the time. Shreve adapted a high-pressure steam engine developed by Oliver Evans in 1801 for use in his flour mill. He installed both the engine and the boilers horizontally on the deck, rather than vertically in the hold as had been the practice. This may have been done for practical reasons, in order to connect the engine to the wheel installed at the stern, but it was a real innovation that was to become standard practice in the construction of future vessels. While the completed boat looked more like a shed than a floating palace, it gave the first indication of the shape and structure that was to make the steamboat such an icon of American history.

The engine Shreve installed in the *Washington*, based on a design by Evans, was a high-pressure engine, lighter in weight and producing about 100 horsepower, more powerful than those used by Fulton. The engine was criticized as being dangerous, which may have been due in part to the concept

Opposite:
A View of St. Louis from Across the River, showing the steamboat *Yellowstone*. This painting, by artist George Catlin in 1832, is one of many he made depicting the western territories and people.

A contemporary illustration of Henry Shreve's steamboat, *Washington*, built in 1825, shows the general construction and shape that was to become characteristic of future boats.

being too advanced for the manufacturing techniques of the time. On a test trip, the *Washington*'s boiler blew up, killing thirteen of its crew and scalding others, including Shreve, who was blown overboard. The explosion was caused when the weight on the safety valve slid by accident to the end of the lever. The boat's owner was not dissuaded, however. He repaired his boat and modified the valve by installing a cam to automatically shut off the steam in its cylinder before the piston completed its cycle.

The *Washington* was launched from Wheeling in May 1816, made its first journey to New Orleans in the spring of 1817 with a cargo, and then returned upriver to Louisville. That return trip took twenty-five days, a remarkable achievement. Livingston's and Fulton's jealous attempts to maintain their monopoly caused them to twice try to seize both the *Enterprise* and the *Washington*, but, not intimidated by their threats, Shreve was able to maintain possession and remain in business.

While *The New Orleans* had shown that steamboat business was possible, Shreve's boats demonstrated it could be a viable concern. Builders and

The Howard Ship Yard at Jeffersonville, Indiana, constructed hulls so well crafted many lasted two years longer than the average five. Hulls 180 to 260 feet long required 100,000 to 225,000 feet of lumber for each hull.

entrepreneurs began burgeoning along the riverbanks as prospective owners sought a share of the trade. The forests were the primary reason boat builders had migrated inland, but there were also coal deposits to fire the smelters used to produce iron for the engines and boilers. Steamboats began to be launched from the banks of the Allegheny and Monongahela rivers at Pittsburgh and from the banks of the Ohio River at Cincinnati and Louisville. Author Louis Hunter calculated the number of steamboats in 1817 to be seventeen, having 3,290 total tonnage. Just twenty-three years later, there were 536 boats with 83,592 tonnage. By 1860, those numbers were 735 boats totaling 162,735 tons.

Free to experiment, builders adopted innovations for their own use or, if they thought they might do better, altered them to suit the needs of the area. This resulted in vast improvements over the original vessels. Their first solution to the problem of draft was to build smaller boats, but their smaller cargo capacity could not meet increasing business demands. While making the boats longer and narrower was not difficult, it took several years, from about 1818 to the 1830s, to create a boat that could carry additional weight, maintain a shallow draft, and yet be structurally sound. Some flexibility was desirable in order for the boat to more easily float over

The Mirror

OF

LITERATURE, AMUSEMENT, AND INSTRUCTION.

No. 679.]   SATURDAY, AUGUST 30, 1834.   [PRICE 2*d.*

AMERICAN STEAM-BOAT.

Drawing of the *Belvidere*, made in the 1830s, is out of proportion, but shows the general features of boats of the time, with sidewheels covered by boxes and two decks. Mrs. Frances Trollope described her experiences on the *Belvedere* in her book about American manners and customs, written in 1828.

The steam towboat *Sprague*, shown in this 1968 photograph, was built in 1901 and operated until decommissioned in 1948. She was 276 feet long with a beam of 61 feet. Note the extensive use of "hog chains." She was nicknamed "Big Mama" because of her massive size.

Postcard showing the sternwheel packet *Alda*, which spent several years on the Missouri River, shown here at Memphis with a load of cotton. The boat was built in 1891, ending her career in the Memphis-Fulton trade.

shoals and sandbars, but the consequences of extreme bowing of the ends or "hogging," which occurred when the bow and stern sagged downward, were obvious. Sometime during the late 1830s, "hog chains" were introduced, iron bars that ran the length of a boat's hull. Attached to braces with a series of turnbuckles, the chains helped prevent the bow and stern from bending. This allowed builders to create more flexible hulls that were more likely to survive when stranded in shallow water. The hog chains were even more important as support for stern-mounted paddlewheels that were

Boat Loaded with Cotton at Wharf, Memphis, Tenn.

Over twice as large as *Alda*, the cotton boat *Henry Frank* ran the Memphis to New Orleans trade. On April 2, 1881, she carried the largest cotton cargo ever brought to New Orleans by a packet: 9,226 bales of cotton and 250 tons of other freight.

increasingly being used. Sternwheels had been used earlier but were enclosed in the hull, giving the hull the shape of a bootjack.

At the time, sidewheel boats were preferred because they gave a smoother ride, were faster, and were more maneuverable. But they were also difficult to manage on the winding turns of the rivers and not as effective in shallow water. Sternwheel boats were able to operate where other boats could not; though not as nimble as their sidewheel brethren, they were easier for the engineers and pilots to manage on the convolutions of the rivers and in the approaches and departures at shallow landings where there were no wharf boats.

The development of the superstructure evolved around the need to balance space for cargo and passengers. The main deck was the place not only for cargo, but also for machinery and the storage of fuel. As the hulls became longer and faster, the width of the main deck floor extended gradually from the bow to the width of the sidewheels. Called guards, these extensions provided some protection from debris for the wheels, but were mainly

During the Civil War, *Jacob Strader* was used to carry sick and injured soldiers. She had a cabin 300 feet long and berths for 310 passengers. Her guards added 69 feet to the width of her main deck to allow for additional freight.

29

Fort Union at the Mouth of the Yellowstone River, 2,000 Miles Above St. Louis was made by George Catlin after the steamboat Yellowstone had reached the settlement in 1832. The many drawings, paintings, and notes made by Catlin are an invaluable record of the time.

intended to provide additional room for cargo. Over time, these guards exceeded the width of the hull by as much as 60 percent to 75 percent. There were exceptions to this, with some larger boats, such as the *Jacob Strader*, a huge boat built in 1853 to run the mail line between Cincinnati and Louisville; the width of her guards extended 69 feet while her beam measured 29.5 feet.

As the boats became more numerous and larger, they also got faster. The record of twenty-five days from New Orleans to Louisville set by *Washington* in 1817 was easily eclipsed by 1825 with boats routinely able to make the round trip to New Orleans, pick up cargo, and return to Louisville in thirty days.

Shreve reported that his first two trips between Louisville and New Orleans paid for the boat and its operating expenses and generated a profit of $1,700 for the shareholders. Another steamboat, *Aetna*, is recorded to have cleared $40,000 during her first season. With returns like that, investors wanted in on the profits and kept the boatyards in production. The boats fanned out onto the tributaries, exploring the frontiers, searching for business.

The first boat to reach St. Louis was the *Zebulon M. Pike*, which was followed by boats whose masters were determined to conquer the Missouri River's infamous shoals, hazards, and drifting riverbed. A military operation consisting of four boats began its journey in June 1819. Only one of the four, the *Western Engineer*, survived; it had been specially designed for the trip, having a sternwheel and drafting just 18 inches. The boat's most unusual feature, though, was its bow. Carved to represent a serpent, smoke poured from its mouth as it proceeded upriver. The boat got as far as Fort Missouri then returned to St. Louis the following spring.

It took decades before steamboat builders accepted that boats meant to run on the Mississippi were not going to work well, if at all, on the "Big Muddy." The American Fur Company sent its own boat, the *Yellowstone*, up the Missouri in 1832, to the mouth of the Yellowstone River. It did not make it until the following year, when the artist Karl Bodmer accompanied the expedition, returning with a series of remarkable paintings and drawings depicting the landscapes and the Native Americans who lived there.

The most successful steamboats were run by Captain Joseph Labarge. He was determined to establish trade on the Missouri and worked for twenty years to do so, beginning in 1839. Every time he ran into a problem on the river, Labarge worked to find solutions and applied them to future boats, building shallow-draft vessels and developing methods to keep the boilers from being ruined by the river's high amount of silt. In 1859, he and his brothers established the navigation head of the Missouri River when they reached the trading post at Fort Benton, Arkansas. Unfortunately, the Civil War would intervene to prevent much growth into the area for several years.

Farther south, Henry Shreve turned his attention to the problem of snags on the rivers. Snaggings were so common they were almost regarded as an inevitability of river travel, accounting for roughly 60 percent of recorded accidents. About 165 miles above where the Red River met the Mississippi was an island of snags 160 miles long. This raft grew continuously, as more driftwood was added to the tangled mass each season. Shreve designed and constructed a large sternwheel boat having a double bow he called a snagboat. Above the bow was a crane-like derrick with an immense parrot-like hook on the end that was used to impale and drag away the built-up debris of the raft. Large snags were retrieved from the river, sawed into manageable pieces,

A bird's-eye view of the St. Louis riverfront, 1859.

Above:
The snagboat
E. A. Woodruff
was built in 1874.
She operated the
entire length of
the Ohio River
during her career,
until retiring from
government
service in
the 1920s.

Right: Steamboats
lined up at the
New Orleans
levee.

and allowed to float harmlessly away. Beginning in 1833, using several snagboats, Shreve and his crews were able to clear the raft in five years.

The average life span of a western river steamboat was five years, far less than that of ocean-going vessels of the time, or even that of the eastern steamboats, which had an average life span of seven years. The reasons for this were many, all based in the fact that the boats had hard lives. If the boat was worked a lot, it may easily have been that insufficient attention was paid to its

A group of
unidentified
men pauses to
have their picture
taken at the stern
of a small harbor
tow. Note the
construction of
the wheel, made
from wood with
iron fittings, and
the hog chains.

Boats iced in
at the Cincinnati
riverfront during
the winter of 1905.
If there happened
to be an ice surge,
boats would be
crushed where
they were tied.

maintenance. In fact, some owners calculated a short life span for the boat as part of their business plan, hiring rough crew and unqualified workers who drove the boat hard, neither expecting nor intending that she last beyond a few years. Given the routine river hazards, fires, and explosions, as well as just plain wearing out, roughly 20 percent of the boats needed to be replaced each year.

The most characteristic feature of the boats, their paddlewheels, were made from wood, with iron strapping used for reinforcement. This was due, in part, to the difficulties in casting iron parts large enough to meet the need. Since the boats often broke down away from populated areas where they could be easily repaired, wood was used because it was generally available everywhere the boat went. If the boat's wheel hit a submerged log, it was easier to replace the shattered paddle than to try to repair a warped and dented piece of iron. Moreover, it was difficult to find skilled workers to do repairs, necessitating that the boat be as easy to work on as possible.

Oliver Evans published *The Abortion of the Young Steam Engineers' Guide* in 1805, and it remained the engineers' bible for many years. The high-pressure engine was not a shiny, attractive piece of engineering, but functional and reliable. Engines were often taken from worn out, wrecked, or sunken boats to be used in new vessels. Precise tolerances were not needed, allowing the engines, boilers, and connections to waste a lot of energy. This was not a concern because the forests were seen as a never-ending source of fuel. The smaller boats consumed up to 24 cords of wood every 24 hours, the larger boats as much as 75 cords each day. A cord of wood is tightly stacked, cut timber 8 feet long, 4 feet high, and 4 feet deep. On long journeys, boats would stop at landings where the deckhands and deck passengers would load additional wood onto the boat.

Small packet shown at the canal landing at Lowell, Ohio, on the Muskingum River near Marietta. Boats such as these provided much-needed service to small towns, bringing supplies to people and transporting their goods and produce to larger markets.

The sternwheel towboat *Iron Age*, with barges near Wheeling, West Virginia. Her chimneys are "broke back" to allow her to safely pass under bridges. The stacks on some boats could rise as high as 75 feet above the water.

Broadside from 1851 detailing the rates for shipping freight and passenger fares for the Cape Fear Steamboat Company.

The vast majority of the vessels were not the floating palaces engraved upon our imaginations, but were instead smaller work-a-day packets that ran daily trades, stopping at landings thirty to forty times each trip to pick up and unload passengers, freight, and livestock. They may not have had sleeping quarters or provided meals, but such packets provided residents in isolated regions transportation to larger towns or just to visit friends and family in the area, well into the twentieth century.

They did, however, share features that were similar, varying according to the pocketbook and ambitions of their owners and the way in which the boat was to be used. The superstructure, including the main deck, was composed of the boiler deck, the hurricane deck, and then the texas deck and the pilothouse, which crowned it all. While the boats did look top heavy, they were, in fact, very stable, with each tier slightly recessed from the one below. The boiler and hurricane decks had sufficient area to allow for a promenade where passengers could get exercise or just sit to watch the scenery. The machinery below had been carefully placed, its weight sitting low enough to counterbalance that of the superstructure. In fact, the walls, partitions, and decorative woodwork were as thin as possible to avoid added weight and were painted white with gilt trim to disguise their flimsiness.

The boats' chimneys were made of iron, riveted in sections to rise up from the furnace, through the decks in front of the pilot house, towering as

The crew of the sternwheel packet *Eclipse* of Evansville, Indiana, has paused in their work to watch some activity outside the frame. The woman on the deck holds a rolling pin, if needed. This *Eclipse* was one of several that shared the name over the years.

The pilothouse of the *Golden Eagle*, built in 1904 as the cotton packet *Wm. Garig*. The boat enjoyed a long career before being sold and remodeled in 1918 to become the passenger and freight packet *Golden Eagle*, and finally was retired in the 1930s.

much as 75 feet above the water. Frequently topped by ornamental crowns, the chimneys both released fiery smoke from the furnaces and drew in cooler air to fan their flames. Ramps were added at the front of the boats for easy access to the landings. The tall staff that arose from the center of the bow was not a flagpole; called a jackstaff, it was used by the pilot as a sighting device so he could tell the boat's position as he guided it along the river.

One of the larger, more ornate boats of the time, *Eclipse* was a sidewheel packet launched from New Albany, Indiana in 1852. She ran the route from Louisville to New Orleans until 1860, when she was severely damaged during a storm and then dismantled.

There is no definite date or specific event one can point to indicating just when the steamboat era came to an end. Some historians place it at the beginning of the Civil War in 1861; others to when the railroad business began to extend their lines during the mid-1850s into areas previously served only by steamboats. Always subject to delays due to river levels and breakdowns, steamboats consistently lost passengers to the more comfortable, convenient, and timely service provided by the railroads. The war brought a discernable decrease, both in travel and in the construction of new boats, as the railroads built lines throughout the North and farmers settled in the Midwest, providing new sources for crops such as wheat and corn. In order to survive, the steamboats gradually adapted their business, turning to towing coal and commodities, operating excursion boats for pleasure cruises, which remain the only vestige of a once thriving piece of American history.

In accordance with the Act of Congress, approved August 30, 1852.

The First Renewal.

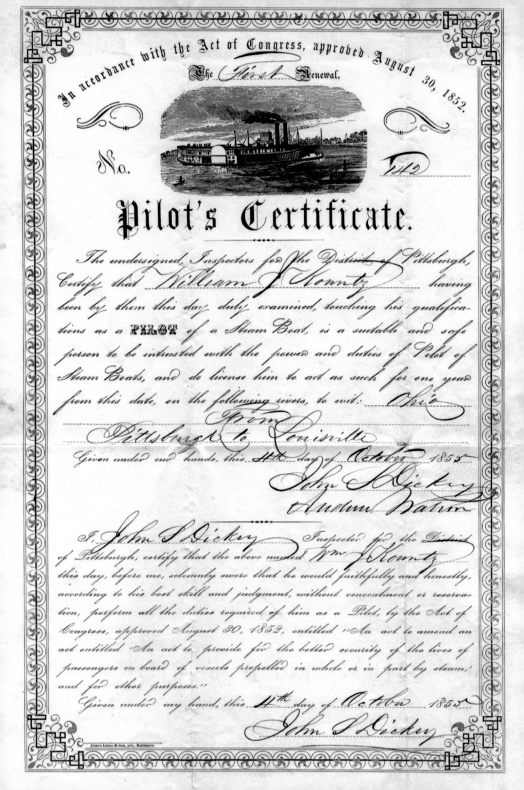

No. __742__

Pilot's Certificate.

The undersigned, Inspectors for the District of Pittsburgh, Certify that __William J Koontz__ having been by them this day duly examined, touching his qualifications as a **PILOT** of a Steam Boat, is a suitable and safe person to be intrusted with the power and duties of Pilot of Steam Boats, and do license him to act as such for one year from this date, on the following rivers, to wit: __Ohio__ __From__ __Pittsburgh to Louisville__

Given under our hands, this __4th__ day of __October__ 1855.

John S Dickey
Andrew Watson

I, __John S Dickey__ Inspector for the District of Pittsburgh, certify that the above named __Wm J Koontz__ this day, before me, solemnly swore that he would faithfully and honestly, according to his best skill and judgment, without concealment or reservation, perform all the duties required of him as a Pilot, by the Act of Congress, approved August 30, 1852, entitled "An act to amend an act entitled 'An act to provide for the better security of the lives of passengers on board of vessels propelled in whole or in part by steam,' and for other purposes."

Given under my hand, this __4th__ day of __October__ 1855.

John S Dickey

James Lucas & Son, prs, Baltimore.

BOAT LIFE

ONE DAY IN 1911, a little boy and his brother stood with their mother, watching the approach of the steamboat that was to take them on a trip from Pittsburgh to Cincinnati. They marveled at *The Queen City*'s white and gold-gilt glory, and its tall, black stacks. Once onboard, the boys climbed the boat's stairs until they reached the pilothouse, the glass-enclosed aerie from which the pilot guided the boat. Forbidden entry, the boys pressed their noses to the window to look inside at the giant wheel used to steer the boat, where the pilot found them as he came to begin his work. He invited the boys to look around inside, and answered myriad questions, until bells outside signaled the pilot to prepare to leave. When he left the pilothouse, Fred Way's destiny was sealed; he would become a steamboat pilot.

Samuel Clemens recounted his time on the river in *Life on the Mississippi*, a book that has fueled the imaginations of countless children and adults since it was published in 1883. He wrote of watching the boats that came to the landing at Hannibal, Missouri, where he and his friends plotted and schemed to find ways to escape their humdrum existence for a life of excitement as a steamboatman. One by one, the boys found their way to the river, with Clemens set on learning to be a pilot.

Originally, owners of flatboats and keelboats employed men who knew the river to take their merchandise and harvests downriver for sale. A pool of men who hired themselves out exclusively as pilots grew out of these undertakings. Nicholas Roosevelt had hired an experienced pilot to take *The New Orleans* on its odyssey, and Henry Shreve was himself a skilled keelboat pilot who drew on his knowledge when he designed and built his own steamboats.

A hierarchy developed that was divided into three classes: officers, made up of the captain, clerk, pilots, engineers, and a mate; the cabin crew, consisting of the cooks, porters, waiters, and maids; and the deck crew, consisting of deckhands and the firemen who stoked the furnaces. Of the officers, all but the pilot generally stayed with the same boat from season to season. The pilot's service was determined by which sections of the river

Opposite:
Pilot's certification issued to William Koontz in 1852, certifying that he had met the qualifications to guide boats on the Ohio River between Pittsburgh and Louisville.

Right: The *Queen City* was designed for an affluent clientele. Built in 1897, her cabin was made from mahogany and had gilt trim. It is said her long career was due in part to her excellent design. She was taken out of service in the 1930s.

Below: Drawing by American illustrator F. C. Yohn for a 1901 issue of *Scribner's* magazine, showing a pilot pulling the cord on his boat's bell.

he was knowledgeable about and licensed to steer; if the boat happened to change its area of operation, then a different pilot was required. The cabin crew was similar in service and skills to those people who worked in hotels or restaurants, but generally only stayed with the same boat for a season. The deckhands

were the "casual" labor of the time. Usually hired on for one trip only, they were recruited at public "shape-ups." Deckhands stowed the cargo in the hold and on the decks, while the roustabouts worked on the levees among the dockworkers.

The role of the captain was in the overall management of the boat. He was the public face of the boat, meeting with the passengers and guests, doing whatever he could to make the boat popular with clients and travelers. Captains needed to know everything about the boat, what was required for the safety of the boat and its passengers, and how to maintain its profitable operation. The captain was likely to have at least some ownership interest in the boat. It was possible for pilots, as well as clerks and mates, to become captains of their own boats.

The pilot was the craftsman of his day, whose skills were acquired through long years of experience. He could understand the boat's behavior on a particular stretch of water and know what was beneath the surface, whether it was a sandbar or snag. He could read the color of the water, the way the ripples formed on the surface. The captain may have been in charge of the boat, but the pilot was in charge once the lines were taken in and the boat backed away from the levee.

There was a division of authority between the two men that may have seemed odd to the outsider, but made sense in practice—if it seemed dangerous to the pilot to take the boat out, he could hold her for any reason: storm, ice, fog, whatever. But if it seemed dangerous to the captain to take the boat out, the pilot could not go. Should a storm hit when they were underway, the pilot did not have to take the boat to shore if he thought it better to remain on the river, but if he wished to land, the captain could not prevent him from doing so. However, neither man ignored any request made by the engineer: If he said the boat needed to be taken to shore, it was done immediately.

Deckhands bringing in the stage as their boat pulls away from the landing.

When Oliver Evans was promoting his high-pressure steam engine, he described one of its main features as its ease of operation and maintenance. While this was a real advantage in a sparsely populated country where it was difficult to obtain parts, it was also a danger, as there were so few qualified men available to run either Evans's engine or the more complicated low-pressure systems. Steam power may have been the cutting-edge technology of the time, but the job of an engineer was hot and greasy, demanding neither respect nor high wages. Between the lack of qualified engineers and low pay, it was frequently necessary to learn on the job.

There was little understanding of the limitations of the engines and boilers. From 1816 to 1848, there were a total of 185 explosions on the western rivers, accounting for 1,443 fatalities. The first steamboat act passed by Congress in 1838 attempted to establish regulations to prevent disasters, such as those of the *Moselle* and *Oronoko*, which exploded in separate incidents in 1838, killing at least 250 people, with many unaccounted for. It was 1852 before a second, stronger steamboat act established laws that required testing of boilers and the use of steam pressure valves. The legislation also established a federal maritime inspection service. Its effect was noticed within a short time, as the number of explosions and fatalities became a fraction of their earlier numbers; for a subsequent year, there were a total of fifteen explosions on the western rivers, with thirteen fatalities.

In 1862, Robert Smalls, a slave who had been contracted by his master to work as a pilot for a Charleston, South Carolina, boat yard, guided the steamboat *Planter* through the Union blockade to free himself, his family, and thirteen friends. Smalls went on to become the first African-American captain of a U.S. vessel and a five-term Congressman.

Deckhands endured brutal working conditions, often with frequent beatings by the mate. They slept on the decks of the boat where they worked, finding their rest on a handy bale of cotton or pile of rags. Only rarely was shelter or bunks provided out of the weather. During cold weather, those who could sought warmth near the machinery, or in the hold. No African-American deckhand could aspire to any position higher than that of steward or barber.

Over time, the image of the bright, lacy boat gracefully riding the rivers faded from the American landscape, evolving into the powerful towboats we see today, to become an icon paying homage to a slower time. Like any icon, it comes dressed in pretty stories that hide a more interesting reality, one that shows the strength and innovation of the people who worked so hard to develop the technology, as well as the existence of ugly prejudices. The steamboat era arrived with the creation of a new government, brought steam power to American shores, and also played a part in the enactment of legislation that sowed the seeds for subsequent regulations related to business behavior, as well as worker and passenger safety.

Captain and pilot Mary Baker Greene greets passengers boarding the *Gordon C. Greene*. The photograph appeared in a 1949 issue of *Holiday* magazine promoting the pleasures of a river trip on one of the Greene Line steamers.

PASSENGERS

WHILE western river steamboats originally were intended for carrying freight, they all had accommodations for passengers. There were two classes on a steamboat: cabin and deck. Cabin passengers had access to a bed and meals; deck passengers had only a ride on the boat, without a bed or food unless they brought it themselves. On these vessels, a clear and dramatic line had been drawn between those who had money and those who didn't.

When Henry Shreve built the *Washington*, he constructed a long room on the main deck with berths along the sides for male passengers. In the stern of the boat, inside the hull, he provided separate accommodations for women. Even though they may have been married, men and women remained in different rooms, and men weren't allowed to enter the women's area without specific permission from the women.

Interior photograph taken in 1860 showing the ladies' cabin on the *Planter*.

Over the years, passenger accommodations were adapted as needed to find room for more freight. By 1840, the basic layout was established and remained approximately the same: Cabin passengers were housed on the boiler deck where a long saloon provided an open room for daytime use. Depending on the size of the boat, sleeping quarters ranged from tiered canvas cots along the sides, screened from view by a curtain, to cabins with dimensions ranging from 5 feet by 7 feet to 12 by 12 feet in size.

The ladies' quarters were, again, at the back of the boat,

separate from the men's. While as far as possible from the heat and danger of the boilers, the women nevertheless had to put up with the vibrations of the wheel. Their lounge was carpeted and may even have had a piano for their amusement. The men's area was not carpeted because a lot of the men did not use the spittoons provided by the boat's staff. Outside, the boiler deck had enough room for passengers to walk the perimeter of the boat and watch the countryside pass by.

The intricate woodwork, paint, and decorations found on the larger, more elaborate boats reflected the wealth and vast resources to be found along the Mississippi River. Merchants ran advertisements in local papers stating they could "furnish entire steamboats ... at short notice." Captains made arrangements with retailers to furnish their boats, referring potential customers from the boat to the stores.

The grand saloon was the hub of social activity for the boat, where one met people of all types, a varied, often colorful, clientele whose crude

Painting of the interior of the main cabin of the steamboat *Imperial* by Louisiana artist Marie Adrian Persac. Though somewhat out of scale, the 1861 gouache and collage painting shows the delicate scrollwork, stained glass, and furnishings available on the better boats. It is the only known depiction of the interior of an antebellum steamboat.

45

Previous pages:
The steamboat
landing at
Vicksburg,
Mississippi, with
the handsome
sidewheeler *Belle
of the Bends* in the
background. She
ran the Greenville-
Vicksburg trade
from 1898 to
about 1909.

Below: Steamboat
"making tow"
near Pennsylvania
coal fields, in
preparation for
moving coal
downriver to
cities, such
as Cincinnati,
Louisville, and
New Orleans.
Coal remains a
vital cargo, taken
by towboats up
and down the
rivers for use by
power companies.

manners both relieved the boredom of the journey and were tiresome and annoying. During the day people gathered in the saloon, visiting with other passengers, reading, or playing card games until they left to allow the stewards to prepare the room for meals. Depending on the size of the boat, a long table may have been set up to allow for a number of seatings, determined by the social hierarchy on the boat. People hovered until the food was placed on tables, then made a mad rush, crowding out the competition, and ate as much as they cared to before the way was cleared for subsequent seatings. On more refined boats, efforts were made to provide more sophisticated service.

Fancy accoutrements were not found just below on the main deck. Passengers who did not have the fare for a stateroom were confined to the deck with cargo, deckhands, and livestock for the duration of their trip. The cheap fare was the only advantage deck passengers enjoyed over those who had paid for a stateroom. They found their beds wherever there might be a free bale of cotton, a row of kegs to stretch out on, or perhaps a patch of bare deck unsoiled by man or beast. No meals were provided other than what they themselves had brought, typically provisions that were not likely to spoil, such as bologna, crackers, and cheese. The only stove on deck was provided both for cooking and to provide warmth.

As the railroads extended their service across the country into areas previously served only by steamboats, business fell off precipitously for the packets. Clerks had to work harder to find cargo at the landings. The mid- to late 1850s began to see a decline in travel because the railroads were able

Steamer "Valley Gem" on the Canal, Zanesville, O. 11526.

Shown in a lock on the Muskingum River, the *Valley Gem* made daily trips between McConnellsville and Zanesville from 1897 to 1917. Boats operating on the Muskingum were built to accommodate the locks, which are part of a lock and dam system built in 1840. Still in operation today, the waterway was designated a National Historic Civil Engineering Landmark by the American Society of Civil Engineers.

to provide regularly scheduled service to both freight and passenger clients. Always subject to delays due to river levels and breakdowns, steamboats consistently lost passengers to the more comfortable, convenient, and timely service provided by the railroads.

With the start of the Civil War in 1861, boatyards along the Ohio River built fewer hulls; most of their clients were from the South come up North with a sketch and a down payment for a new hull—"make her just like the last one, but with a bigger cash drawer"—but business did not return to its prewar form. Although boats continued to be built, they were fewer in number and smaller as boat owners adapted to the economic changes. The structure of the boats was altered: Sternwheelers became more husky as they were increasingly used to tow barges of coal; packets were adapted to carry less freight and more passengers; while other boats became excursion vessels, introducing the public to the concept of pleasure rides. Overall, the postwar years brought an increase in passenger service, even as the freight business fell off.

The 1890s saw the introduction of the first steel-hulled packets. The *Kate Adams*, launched from the Howard Ship Yards at Jeffersonville, Indiana, in 1898, ushered in a gradual transition from the production of wooden hulls, the resources for which were becoming increasingly difficult to obtain and more expensive. Forests for miles around had been denuded as builders cut down large stands of mature yellow pine for the hulls. At first, steel hulls were only occasionally built, but as the yards had to go increasingly far afield to find high-quality wood free of knots, steel became the material of choice. The last packet built by the Howards was the *Cape Giradeau*, which came off the ways in 1923. The boat worked hauling both freight and passengers until 1935,

Steel hulls in
the process
of construction
in 1885 at the
Rees Shipyards
at Pittsburgh.
The company
built boats for the
South American
market.

In 1922, a bucket
of tar being heated
on the galley stove
was overturned,
setting fire to the
Morning Star, which
spread to other
boats tied at
the Cincinnati
wharves, including
the *Island Queen*,
the *Tacoma*, and
the *Chris Greene*.

when she was bought and converted for passenger use alone, joining the Greene Line family of steamers at their base in Cincinnati on the Ohio River.

The Greene Line was started in 1890 by Gordon Greene when he bought the *H. K. Bedford*, a packet then working on the Cumberland River. Greene and his wife Mary Baker Greene were known to be tough but fair, successfully maintaining their packet line when others were going bankrupt. Their reputation for fairness earned them the respect of everyone along the rivers. When Captain Greene died in 1927, his coffin was borne upriver to Newport on the *Tom Greene*, with thousands of people paying tribute as the boat passed.

Chris Greene, their eldest son, was expected to take over the business, which he did until his death at age forty-three from a heart attack. Captain Greene thought his younger son, Tom, was too much of a dreamer to effectively run the company, but it was Tom Greene's inspiration that brought the Greene Line continued success. Over the years, the Greene boats increasingly concentrated on passenger service, providing

In this photograph from a 1949 issue of *Holiday* magazine, "Mack Davis, Headwaiter, and Ray, the Pantryman, chat while serving salad at a meal" on board the *Gordon C. Greene*. The pictures were part of an article about vacation cruises on the river.

inexpensive pleasure trips during World War II, a time when sacrifices made for the war effort limited people's travel. After the war, Tom Greene decided to buy a large packet from the West Coast he thought would sustain the company after the wartime freight business had fallen off.

Offered at public sale in late 1946 by the U.S. Maritime Commission, the *Delta Queen*, along with her sister boat, the *Delta King*, had been used by the U.S. Navy as yard ferry boats in San Francisco Bay. The boats ran a scheduled service from 1926 to 1940 between San Francisco and Sacramento, when the completion of a highway between the two cities left them idle until commandeered by the Navy after the attack on Pearl Harbor. Greene's bid of $46,250 won him the *Delta Queen*, a boat that had cost its original owner $875,000 to build.

The towboat *Titan* was built in 1930 by the Howard Ship Yards. The steel-hulled vessel, owned by the Jones & Laughlin Steel Company, operated on the upper Ohio River and remained active until she was sold for scrap in 1953.

Guests enjoying dinner aboard the *Gordon C. Greene* in 1949. Captain Mary can be seen seated at right, seeming to keep an eye on the photographer.

Captain Tom prevailed on his friend, Fred Way, himself a steamboat captain as well as the author of such books as *The Log of the Betsy Ann*, to bring the *Delta Queen* to the Ohio River. In San Francisco, Captain Way found

Brochures promoting vacation trips on the Greene Line steamboats.

The *Delta Queen*, photographed during a stop at Paducah, Kentucky.

This scene from the early 1900s shows a small steamboat with "lighters" full of baled cotton. These small lighters often were used for extra fuel for the boats or extra cargo, eventually evolving into the towboat business on the rivers today.

the boat moored among other decommissioned vessels, all painted gray. She was towed to the Fulton Shipyard and prepared for sea. With her flat-bottomed hull, the boat would never survive the ocean waves, so Way had her exterior clad in unpainted wood. Looking like a massive shipping crate, the *Delta Queen* was slowly towed by tugboat from San Francisco, down the Pacific Coast to the Panama Canal. She was then taken up the Gulf Coast

The *Gordon C. Greene* is shown during a 1949 excursion on the Mississippi River near Prairie du Chien, Wisconsin.

to Harvey, Louisiana, and put in operating condition. From there, Captain Way piloted her to the Dravo Shipyard at Neville, Pennsylvania, where she underwent extensive upgrades and repairs in preparation for her career on the Ohio, Mississippi, Cumberland, and Tennessee rivers.

On March 1, 1948 the *Delta Queen* debuted as part of the Greene Line, operating for the next sixty years and becoming a much-loved icon by the people who worked on her, rode her, or just watched her pass by. Captain Mary Greene was among the first people to move aboard. She had become a legend, a gracious and generous woman who enjoyed meeting the people who came aboard the boat to hear stories of her river life. She died aboard the *Queen* about a year later, and it has been said her ghost still inhabits her suite. Captain Tom died suddenly as well, of a heart attack in 1950, aged forty-two, while in command of the boat he worked so hard to bring to the western rivers.

Captains Tom Greene and Fred Way, friends since they were young men, participated in three staged steamboat races, 1928–30, between the *Betsy Ann*, the *Tom Greene*, and the *Chris Greene*. This picture is from the 1929 race, which many thought the *Betsy Ann* had won, but *Tom Greene* was declared the winner.

Overleaf:
An everyday scene at the Memphis landing on the Mississippi River, the *Belle of the Bends* in the foreground, with crews loading cargo as passengers board with their luggage.

In 1962, an amendment to the Safety of Life at Sea Act was passed by the International Maritime Organization that, generally speaking, forbade the operation of a commercial vessel having a wooden superstructure and carrying fifty or more passengers. Despite the fact that the *Delta Queen* only operated on the rivers of the United States within half a mile of most riverbanks, had every safety upgrade available installed, and that most of her cabins opened to the outside deck, the wooden elements of her superstructure meant she was in violation of the act. Until 2008, she had received exemptions signed by the President of the United States to remain in service. When that exemption was not signed, the boat's career was essentially over.

In 2008, the *Delta Queen* docked at Chattanooga for the last time. After having put her final passengers ashore at Memphis, she was brought to Chattanooga to begin life as a boutique hotel.

FURTHER READING

Allen, Michael. *Western Rivermen, 1763–1861: Ohio and Mississippi Boatmen and the Myth of the Alligator Horse*. 1990: Louisiana State University Press, Baton Rouge.

Andrist, Ralph K. *Steamboats on the Mississippi*. 1962: American Heritage Publishing Co, Inc., New York.

Audubon, John James. *Delineations of American Scenery and Character*. 1926: G. A. Baker & Company. New York.

Baxter, Maurice G. *The Steamboat Monopoly: Gibbons v. Ogden, 1824*. 1972: Alfred A. Knopf, New York.

Bernstein, Peter L. *Wedding of the Waters: The Erie Canal and the Making of a Great Nation*. 2005: W. W. Norton & Company, New York.

Buchanan, Thomas C. *Black Life on the Mississippi: Slaves, Free Blacks, and the Western Steamboat World*. 2004: The University of North Carolina Press, Chapel Hill.

Burke, James. *Connections*. 1978: Little, Brown and Company, Boston.

Busch, Jason T., Monkhouse, Christopher, and Whitmore, Janet L. *Currents of Change: Art and Life Along the Mississippi River, 1850–1861*. The Minneapolis Institute of Arts, Minneapolis, Minnesota.

Clamorgan, Cyprian. Edited with an Introduction by Julie Winch. *The Colored Aristocracy of St. Louis*. 1999: University of Missouri Press, Columbia.

Dohan, Mary Helen. *Mr. Roosevelt's Steamboat: The First Steamboat to Travel the Mississippi*. 1981: Dodd, Mead & Company, New York.

Donovan, Frank. *River Boats of America: From Flatboats to Floating Palaces, From the Cotton Blossom to the Staten Island Ferry*. 1966: Thomas Y. Crowell Company, New York.

Drago, Harry Sinclair. *The Steamboaters: From the Early Sidewheelers to the Big Packets*. 1967: Bramhall House, New York.

Eskew, Garnett Laidlaw. *The Pageant of the Packets: A Book of American Steamboating*. 1929: Henry Holt & Company, New York.

Feldman, Jay. *When the Mississippi Ran Backwards: Empire, Intrigue, Murder, and the New Madrid Earthquakes*. 2005: Free Press, New York.

Fishbaugh, Charles Preston. *From Paddle Wheels to Propellers: The Howard Ship Yards of Jeffersonville in the Story of Steam Navigation on the Western Rivers*. 1970: The Indiana Historical Society, Indianapolis.

Flexner, James Thomas. *Steamboats Come True: American Inventors in Action*. 1944, 1992: Fordham University Press, New York.

Gould, Emerson W. *Fifty Years on the Mississippi: Or Gould's History of River Navigation*. 1889: Nixon-Jones Printing Company, St. Louis.

Halfman, Janet. *Seven Miles to Freedom: The Robert Smalls Story*. 2008: Lee & Low Books, New York.

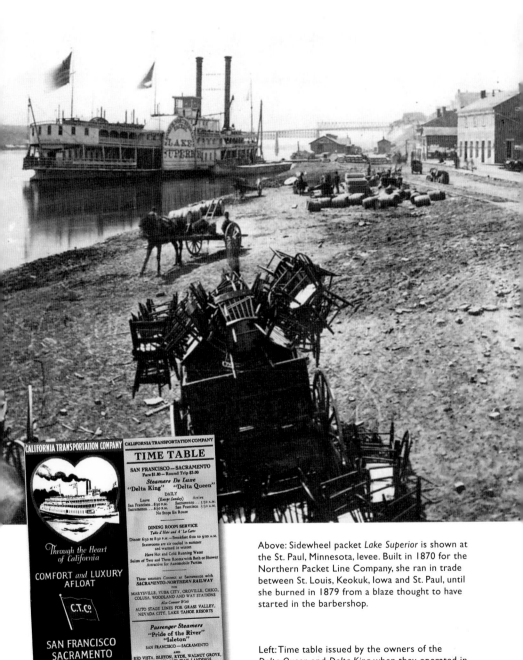

Above: Sidewheel packet *Lake Superior* is shown at the St. Paul, Minnesota, levee. Built in 1870 for the Northern Packet Line Company, she ran in trade between St. Louis, Keokuk, Iowa and St. Paul, until she burned in 1879 from a blaze thought to have started in the barbershop.

Left: Time table issued by the owners of the *Delta Queen* and *Delta King* when they operated in California, between Sacramento and San Francisco.

Sternwheel boats lined up at the Marietta, Ohio, levee for the 2008 Ohio River Sternwheel Festival. Held annually the weekend after Labor Day, the celebration offers entertainment, the Harry J. Robinson fireworks display, and the Captain James E. Sands Memorial races.

Huber, Leonard V. *Advertisements of Lower Mississippi River Steamboats, 1812–1920*. 1959: The Steamship Historical Society of America, Inc., West Barrington, Rhode Island.

Hunter, Louis C. *Steamboats on the Western Rivers: An Economic and Technological History*. 1949, 1977, 1993: Dover Publications, Inc., New York.

Johnson, Paul. *A History of the American People*. 1997: HarperCollins Publishers, Inc., New York.

Kane, Adam I. *The Western River Steamboat*. 2004: Texas A&M University Press, College Station, Texas.

Latrobe, Charles H. *The Rambler in North America*. 1835: Harper & Bros., New York.

Latrobe, John H. B. *A Lost Chapter in the History of the Steamboat*. 1871: Maryland Historical Society, Baltimore.

Latrobe, John H. B. *First Steamboat Voyage on the Western Waters*. 1871: The Maryland Historical Society, Baltimore.

Maristier, Jean Baptiste. *Memoir on Steamboats of the United States of America*. 1824, 1957: The Marine Historical Association, Mystic, Connecticut.

The *Delta Queen* is clad in wood for her ocean voyage. Her Navy designation as *YFB-56* has been painted over and her original name restored.

Paskoff, Paul F. *Troubled Waters: Steamboat Disasters, River Improvements, and American Public Policy, 1821–1860*. 2007: Louisiana State University Press, Baton Rouge.

Rhodes, Richard. *John James Audubon: The Making of an American*. 2004: Vintage Books, New York.

Rosen, William. *The Most Powerful Idea in the World*. 2010: Random House, New York.

Steele, Eliza R. *A Summer Journey in the West*. 1841: John S. Taylor & Company, New York.

Lorena, a well-known packet, ran the Pittsburgh-Zionsville trade from 1895 to 1915. In this picture, she is shown at a wharf boat on the Ohio River in 1908.

Sutcliffe, Andrea. *Steam: The Untold Story of America's Greatest Invention*. 2004: Palgrave Macmillan, New York.

Twain, Mark. *Life on the Mississippi*. 2009: Signet Classic, division of Penguin Group, New York.

Way, Frederick, Jr. *Pilotin' Comes Natural*. 1943: Farrar & Rinehart, Inc., New York.

Way, Frederick, Jr. *The Log of the Betsy Ann*. 1933: Robert M. McBride & Company, New York.

Way, Frederick, Jr. *Way's Packet Directory, 1848–1994*. 1983: Ohio University Press, Athens, Ohio.

ARTICLES

Hulbert, Archer B. "Western Ship-building," July 1916, *American Historical Review*, Vol. XXI, No. 4, pp. 720–733.

Nichols, George Ward. "Down the Mississippi," November 1870, *Harpers New Monthly Magazine*, New York.

Travis, Irven. "Muskingum River Pilots," October 1917, *Ohio Archeological and Historical Quarterly*, Vol. XXVI, No. 4.

WEBSITES

Inland Riverboats Photograph Collection of the Cincinnati and Hamilton County Public Library
http://wiki.cincinnatilibrary.org/index.php/Inland_Riverboats_Photographs_Collection

Historic Steamboat Photographs, University of Wisconsin at LaCross
www.uwlax.edu/murphylibrary/departments/photos.html

PLACES TO VISIT

MUSEUMS

Hannibal History Museum, 217 N. Main Street, Hannibal, Missouri 63401.
Website: www.hannibalhistorymuseum.com

Howard Steamboat Museum, Jeffersonville, Indiana.
Website: www.steamboat.org

Mark Twain Boyhood Home and Museum, 120 N. Main Street, Hannibal, Missouri 63401. Website: www.marktwainmuseum.org

Mississippi River Museum, Mud Island River Park, Memphis, Tennessee.
Website: www.mudisland.com/c-3-mississippi-river-museum.aspx

National River Museum & Aquarium, Dubuque, Iowa.
Website: www.mississippirivermuseum.com

Ohio River Museum, Marietta, Ohio. Website: www.campusmartius.org
Point Pleasant River Museum, Point Pleasant, West Virginia.
  Website: www.pprivermuseum.com
The Steamboat Arabia, Kansas City, Missouri. Website: www.1856.com

ASSOCIATIONS

Sons and Daughters of Pioneer Rivermen was organized in 1939
  "to perpetuate the memory of Pioneer Rivermen and for the
  preservation of river history." Website: www.s-and-d.org
The Historic Sternwheeler Preservation Society, Inc. has as its purpose
  "To preserve, research and promote the heritage and historical
  significance of sternwheel vessels." Website: www.hspsi.org
American Sternwheel Association was established in 1976 to "keep alive
  that precious bit of Americana, the Paddlewheel Riverboat."
  Website: www.americansternwheel.org

STEAMBOAT CRUISES

Str. *Belle of Louisville*, 401 West River Road, Louisville, Kentucky 40202.
  Website: www.belleoflouisville.com
Str. *Natchez*, New Orleans Steamboat Company, 40 N. Peters Street,
  New Orleans, Louisiana 70130. Website: www.steamboatnatchez.com
Str. *American Queen*, American Queen Steamboat Company,
  40 S. Main Street, 21st Flr., Memphis, Tennessee 38103.
  Website: www.americanqueensteamboatcompany.com

A flotilla of sternwheel boats approaches the lock at Hannibal, Ohio, on their way to a festival at Wheeling, West Virginia. Hundreds of such boats are scattered about the country. Owners of these vessels value the relatively slow pace of the journey, taking pleasure in the experience and the scenery.

INDEX

Page numbers in italics refer to illustrations